First edition for the United States, its territories and dependencies, the Philippines, and Canada published in 2006 by Barron's Educational Series, Inc.

First edition for Great Britain published 2006 by Hodder Children's Books, a division of Hodder Headline Limited.

All inquiries should be addressed to:
Barron's Educational Series, Inc.
250 Wireless Boulevard
Hauppauge, New York 11788
http://www.barronseduc.com

Library of Congress Catalog Card No. 2004116975

ISBN-13: 978-0-7641-3212-4
ISBN-10: 0-7641-3212-1

Printed in China
9 8 7 6 5 4 3 2 1

My Manners Matter

A FIRST LOOK AT BEING POLITE

PAT THOMAS

ILLUSTRATED BY LESLEY HARKER

BARRON'S

Have you ever heard someone say "mind your manners"? Do you know what that means?

Manners are the ways we treat others and how we act in public. Good manners show both kindness and respect to people you know – and to people you may not know.

When we have good manners we are polite
and we follow certain rules that make us more
enjoyable to be around.

People can tell if you have good manners by the way you talk and by the way you act. Manners show courtesy.

Good manners are like magic, because when we are well behaved it makes special things happen.

Please?

Saying "please" can make others more willing to help us.

Saying "thank you" makes other people feel good about what they have done.

Saying "I'm sorry" when you have hurt someone can make both of you feel happier.

Lots of people think it's important to behave well only on special occasions.

But, really, we should be practicing good manners every day, with everyone we meet.

Opening the door for someone else, congratulating the winning team, or offering your seat to someone who is not as strong or as healthy as you are all good ways of showing what good manners you have.

So is not making noise when others are trying to work or listen.

What about you?
Can you think of some magic words that show how polite you are? Can you think of some ways to be helpful and polite?

How you behave at the table or on the phone is also important.

Sitting up straight, not talking with your mouth full, and saying "thank you" for a nice meal is always polite.

So is speaking clearly and politely on the phone.

Some people are always being rude. They think people will respect them if they act tough and inconsiderate. It's hard to be polite to them, but try anyway.

Rude people are often very lonely people –
nobody likes to spend time with them because
they hurt other people's feelings and take the
fun out of everything.

A long time ago people had many different ideas about what good manners were.

Children were considered rude if they spoke to an adult without being asked to, or if they didn't stand up every time their teacher came into the room.

Some of these ideas seem silly now,
and lots of ideas about being polite
have changed over the years.

But some ideas are always good — like taking turns, not pushing or shoving, playing fair, asking before you take something, and covering your mouth when you sneeze.

What about you?

Why do you think it's important to practice good manners? Can you say why it is a good idea to ask before you take something that doesn't belong to you?

People from different cultures may have different rules about manners.

Older people may also have been brought up with different ideas about what it means to be polite and how children should behave.

It's important to try to understand these differences and show respect for them.

It doesn't matter whether there are just two of you playing or working together or whether you are in a big group like in the classroom or the playground.

Manners are important wherever you are because being polite makes working and playing together more enjoyable for everyone.

HOW TO USE THIS BOOK

Even though character building is a hot educational topic, manners generally receive little attention in schools. With growing demands on teaching time, manners and etiquette are usually abandoned in favor of teaching the "three R's." While manners today are definitely more casual than in the past, if parents want their children to get by in "polite society" they need to make the effort to teach politeness and respect in a deliberate, intentional way.

Explain to your children why manners are important. They need to hear from you that these rules are important not simply as codes to live by but as acts of kindness and consideration for others.

Teaching your children manners also gives them lifelong survival skills such as self-esteem and self-confidence. Your children learn manners (along with many other character traits) from you. Do your best to speak politely and always treat them and others with kindness and consideration. Teach children to practice common courtesy by writing thank-you notes for gifts, sending thoughtful letters or e-mails to friends and relatives, and remembering birthdays, holidays, and those who are elderly or ill.

Social skills are complex, and with young children it's best to take a step-by-step approach. The first lesson for all children should be using time-honored "magic words" such as "please" and "thank you." Gradually add more examples such as "you're welcome" and "pardon me?" and "may I..." For table manners, work on one or two at a time. On the telephone, encourage clear "hellos" and "good-byes" first, then teach asking the caller to "Please wait a minute while I get my dad." Teach children to take messages.

Teachers can help by instigating discussions about everyday manners and ways to handle ourselves in tricky situations. Ask children to come up with solutions to problems such as: If someone is rude to you, how do you respond? If someone gives you a present that you don't like, what should you say?

Schools provide ample opportunities for children to practice good manners. When a theater company comes to the school and puts on a play, or the local police officer or firefighter comes to talk to the children, ask the students to write thank you e-mails or notes and say what they enjoyed about the visit. If you have a school fair or cake sale, have the children write short notes to thank the organizers – often busy parents who could use some appreciation.

BOOKS TO READ

Madeline Says Merci: The Always Be Polite Book
John Bemelmans Marciano (Viking, 2001)

Oops! Excuse Me, Please! and Other Mannerly Tales
Bob McGrath, Tammie Lyon (Barron's Educational Series, 1998)

The Bad Good Manners Book
Babette Cole (Puffin Books, 1997)

Manners Can Be Fun
Munro Leaf (Universe Publishing, 2004)

What Do You Say, Dear?
Sesyle Joslin, Maurice Sendak (HarperCollins, 1958)

RESOURCES FOR PARENTS

Multicultural Manners: New Rules of Etiquette for a Changing Society
Norine Dresser (Wiley, 1996)

Teaching Your Children Good Manners: A Go Parents! Guide
Lauri Berkenkamp, Steven C. Atkins (Nomad Press, 2001)

365 Manners Kids Should Know
Sheryl Eberly (Three Rivers Press, 2001)

www.emilypost.com
Web site of the Emily Post Institute. Founded by the doyenne of manners in America, this site provides answers to your everyday etiquette questions and manners issues.